1997

RETIREMENT:

**YOUR REWARD FOR
NEVER HAVING
STRANGLED
THE BOSS.**

Dear Mrs. Diez,
I hope that you
have a wonderful
retirement. You deserve it!
Bonne chance!
Lauren Bello
H.H.S. 1/6

DESIGN: MARK EIMER;
PHOTOGRAPHY AND DIGITAL IMAGING: TODD BALFOUR

WRITTEN BY:

Chris Brethwaite, Bill Bridgeman,

Bill Gray, Marn Jensen, Allyson Jones,

Kevin Kinzer, Mark Oatman,

Dee Ann Stewart, Dan Taylor

and Myra Zirkle.

Retirement opens up a whole

new area of irresponsibilities.

Your obligation as a retiree is

to have as much fun as possible.

Your former co-workers are

counting on you.

When you get sentimental

about work, just remember the

in-box from hell.

Never miss an opportunity to

skip something you didn't really

want to do.

Welcome to a world where 9 to 5

is just a baseball score.

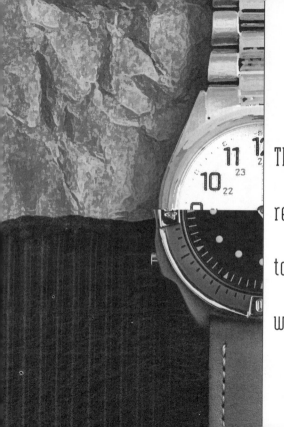

The best part of being on a

retirement cruise is being

totally surrounded by people

who have to work really hard.

If you've pawned your gold

watch for green fees, you may

be playing too much golf.

From now on, it just doesn't matter if you have a clean shirt to match your tie.

Spend a little quiet time with

your grandchildren. No, wait.

That would be impossible.

Never again will it take over

an hour for the clock to move

from 4:55 to 5:00.

It's time to stop working

like a dog and start

sleeping like one.

Go into consulting. First,

consult a road map for the best

route to someplace warm.

Monday, Monday…now you can

trust that day.

If you take up tennis, hire a

kid to jump the net.

Think of retirement as just that

much more time for talk radio.

Perhaps the greatest joy of

retirement is never having to

make an appearance in shorts

at the company picnic.

Enjoy your new position –

horizontal in a hammock.

Never again will you have to wait until evening to read the morning paper.

Retirement is a good time

to get close to family. Or, if you

prefer, really, really far away

from family.

Try some volunteer work.

Voluntarily do whatever the

heck you want.

Now that it doesn't matter

when you get up, you're wide

awake at 5 a.m.

Time to start your new career

in grandchild-spoiling.

Now you can complain about

the government full time.

Retirement requires some adjustments. But a pro can usually work out the kinks in your swing.

Never put off until tomorrow

something you would really just

enjoy the heck out of today.

Nobody ever said retirement

was easy. Well, except

retired people.

Say good-bye to vending

machine coffee forever.

You deserve any discount

you receive.

Retirement is a big step-

Hopefully onto a golf course

or boat dock.

Show your grandkids how to

work in the garden.

Your former co-workers

will miss you. Drop by in

jeans around 10 a.m. to tell

them all about the great day

you've planned.

One good thing about retirement is setting your own goals. For example, one day your goal might be blocking the sun with a big, floppy hat.

Pick a hobby that kind of

bugs your spouse.

Happiness is not needing to care

if a store has evening hours.

Stopping to smell the flowers

is a lot easier when you actually

have time to grow some.

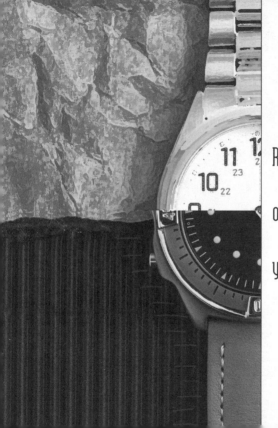

Retirement is nature's way

of saying, "Why didn't I do this

years ago?"

Get to know your grandkids

favorite TV shows.

The first year is the hardest.

But, don't worry...eventually

the new person in your job will

learn to fake replacing you.

There's a very good reason

why alarm clocks aren't

common retirement gifts.

Now you get to decide what part of the country you really want to live in.

Try to get at least out the

door and down the block

before the company falls

apart without you.

When you pack up all your

stuff on the last day of work,

leave the stress there.

Why do they give you a gold

watch now that you don't have

to care what time it is?

The fish don't care if you

wear a tie.

Once you're retired, you

discover that you didn't really

give the company the best years

of your life after all.

If you've done everything you

saved to do for your retirement

years in the first week, you

might want to slow down a bit.

It may take awhile to get used

to not having supervisors take

credit for everything you do.

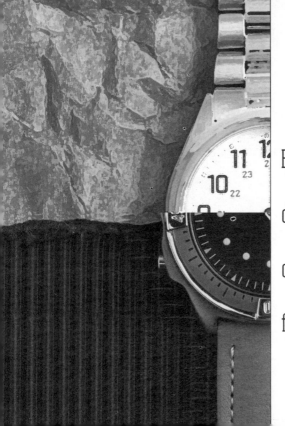

End the speculation. Go from desk to desk showing your co-workers the amount on your final paycheck.

Finally, you have time to

figure out your VCR.

From now on, you don't have to

try to do even one thing at once

if you don't feel like it.

The most important thing to

demonstrate to your grandkids

is a sincere love of life.

Now all of your hats can be

fishing hats.

Before you moon the office,

remember: Your butt's not what

it used to be.

A long weekend can be as

long as you want.

Spread some juicy rumors

about yourself around work so

they'll be talking about you long

after you leave.

Suddenly, the cheap show at the

movies is real convenient.

Congratulations on becoming

one of the idle rich.

Well, except for the rich part.

Retirement is when you

become the person whose grass

is always greener.

You can take the "I'd rather be

fishing" bumper sticker off your

car now.

Retirement: That special time

when you see how long it takes

to go through all the office

supplies you swiped.

Get first shot at weekend garage

sales that start on Friday.

The question every retiree

must answer: "Now what do I

do for aggravation?"

You never have to read

another memo.

Another nice thing about

being retired is that your

refrigerator won't cheat you

out of a quarter.

Retirement is the

all-you-can-eat

buffet of life.

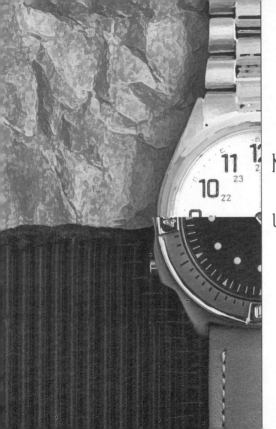

Now you never have to wonder

what was on the late, late show.

About the only reason

you'll have to watch the clock

is if you're cooking a

three-minute egg.

Retirement is a good time to test

all the scout cookie flavors.

There still won't be enough

hours in the day, but the ones

there are will be happier.

From now on, the only

paperwork you'll have to fill

out will be a golf scorecard.

Find out what's in all those

magazines you subscribe to.

Now you can laugh out loud when someone younger says something stupid, instead of saying "Good point! And I'd say that even if you weren't the boss's nephew!"

Read the novel and see

the movie.

Retirement brings freedom...

freedom to wear shorts all day,

freedom to read books all day,

freedom to chuckle at your good

fortune all day...

Always do your yard work

early in the morning, so you can

wave to your neighbors leaving

for the office.

Retirement is a fine kettle of

fish. If you're lucky.

The best thing about those

ponderous classics you always

intended to read after retirement

is that you don't have to read

them if you don't want to.

Learn a new language and visit

someplace where they speak it.

Take time to be romantic again.

Golf shoes and sneakers seldom

need to be shined.

Take a class that has absolutely

no practical application.

Listen to a concert in the park:

The symphony of nature, the

song of the birds, the music of

childrens' laughter.

Actually go to a reunion instead

of just intending to.

Think of retirement as a huge, extended bonus from the company.

You never have to wolf down

breakfast in the car again.

The rabbits on your block would

like for you to start a garden.

Master a video game just to

impress the grandkids.

The first thing on your list of things to do should be to never make another list.

There's no such thing

as a bad nap.

Old neckties make great

kite tails.

The best thing about retirement

is everything.